For Reference

Not to be taken from this room

People of the California Gold Rush

People of the California Gold Rush

Adam D. Parker

Toucan Valley Publications, Inc.

ISBN 1-884925-82-0

Illustrated by Jean Tamminga.

Available from:

Toucan Valley Publications, Inc.
PO Box 15520
Fremont CA 94539-2620

Phone: (800) 236-7946
Fax: (888) 391-6943
E-mail: query@toucanvalley.com

www.toucanvalley.com

Manufactured in the United States of America
First Edition

People of the California Gold Rush

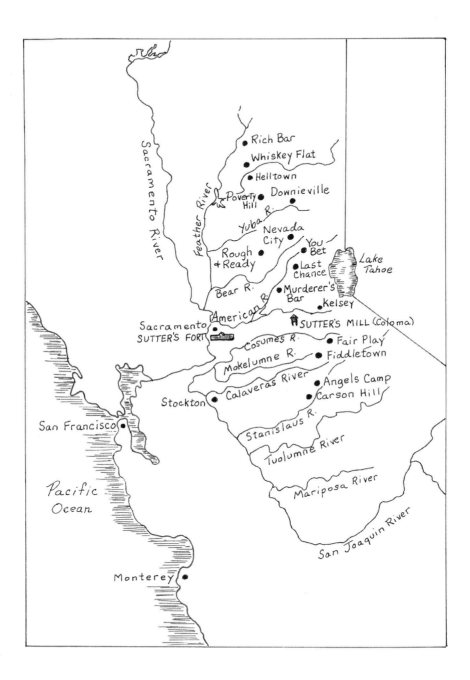

Introduction

When James Marshall found gold in 1848 at Sutter's Mill, the course of California history was forever changed. People from all over the world rushed to California, hoping to strike it rich. The streams of gold-seekers included a great variety of people, each with his or her unique skills. A few found enough gold to make them rich. Most did not. Many disappointed miners took what was left of their money and their hopes and turned back home. Others stayed, however, and their ideas and talents helped shape the future of California.

Most of the gold-seekers were men who had left their families behind. In fact, the lack of women and children in the gold fields helped enhance the fame of those, like dancer Lotta Crabtree and writer Louise Clappe, who were there.

Some of the men who came to California were already successful artists or businessmen. While they hoped to find gold, people like chocolate maker Domingo Ghirardelli and artist Charles Nahl found that the talents they brought with them to California, rather than gold, brought them wealth.

California during the gold rush was also a time of fear and suspicion. Indeed, harsh conditions and the desire for quick wealth led to a great rise in crime. Hence, the bandit Joaquín Murieta became one of the most famous figures of his day. But Murieta's story, as well as that of Mary Ellen Pleasant, shows the prejudice faced by Californians who did not have white skin. This is part of the gold rush story as well.

The gold rush was an exciting, important time in California's history. Gold created new heroes and villains, wealthy leaders and poor souls. But more than anything, it turned America's, and the world's, attention to California. The people who came to the state enriched it with their ideas and enthusiasm. California today would look much different if no one had ever spotted the shiny metal that we call gold.

John Sutter
(1803-1880)

John Sutter's name will always be linked with the California gold rush. Sutter's Fort and Sutter's Mill will always be remembered for the discovery of gold. For John Sutter, however, the discovery of gold signaled the beginning of the end of his dream for California. The gold rush made many people rich, but John Sutter was not one of them.

Early Life

He was born Johann August Suter in Germany in 1803 to Swiss parents. He grew up in Switzerland, where he learned to be a printer. In 1826, he married Annette Dubeld and, the following day, she gave birth to their first child. Johann spent a few years in the Swiss military and rose to the rank of Lieutenant. Then, with money from Annette's mother, he set up a business selling dry goods. Suter was a poor businessman and, by 1834, owed money to many people. Afraid of going to jail because he could not pay his debts, Suter left the country, abandoning his wife and five children.

He soon arrived in America and changed his name to the more English-sounding John Sutter. Sutter spent the next several years in various parts of the United States. He became a trader on the Santa Fe Trail, met many trappers, explored fishing areas in the Pacific Northwest, and journeyed to Hawaii. When he got to California in 1839, he was convinced that his travels had ended.

Sutter's Fort

Sutter came to California with a number of letters of introduction and a somewhat exaggerated story about his own background. He became a Mexican citizen. He asked the Mexican governor of California, Juan Bautista Alvarado, to grant him about 50,000 acres in the area where the Sacramento and American rivers meet. There, Sutter planned to set up a Swiss-style colony called New Helvetia. The governor hoped that he would help protect California from American settlers and hostile Indians.

Sutter built a great complex that he hoped would become a center of business for the area. In 1841, when the Russians abandoned Fort Ross, Sutter bought the buildings and equipment and used them to help construct his fort. Using mostly borrowed money, Sutter tried to create his own empire. Sutter and his men grew grain and fruit, raised cattle, made brandy and wine, and trapped fur. Perhaps most importantly, Sutter welcomed an increasing number of American visitors to his land. Rather than trying to stop people from coming to California, Sutter was far more interested in selling them goods and making a profit.

Labor

Like most large enterprises run by Europeans in the West, Sutter's Fort depended primarily on Indian labor. Sutter recruited hundreds of Indians to work for him, and he treated them badly. While other Europeans and many Americans knew Sutter as a generous man, the Indians he employed often suffered beatings and other harsh treatment.

For the most part, Sutter paid his Indian workers in small metal pieces that could only be used at Sutter's own store. In that way, he was guaranteed to make a good profit. Sutter also set his prices very high, so that the laborers had to work for about two weeks to earn enough to buy a shirt.

Not all of Sutter's Indian workers were paid badly; some were not paid at all. Sutter sometimes had the Indians who worked for him capture members of other tribes. These Indians became slaves who worked his land and were sometimes rented out or sold to other businesses.

In addition to Indian labor, free and unfree, Sutter employed a variety of skilled European, American, and Mexican workers as carpenters and technicians. One of those men, James Marshall, would be the first to discover gold.

Gold!

On January 24, 1848, James Marshall was working on a sawmill at Coloma on the American River when he discovered bits of a yellow metal lying in the water. Sutter's tests proved that the metal was not pyrite or something else of low value. Marshall had indeed discovered gold. Sutter tried to keep this amazing discovery a secret because he feared that too many people would come and destroy his careful plans for the colony he was trying to create.

Sutter, however, underestimated the impact of the discovery. Although he told his workers that they could look for gold in their free time, he did not realize that with such wealth nearby, few of his men would see any value in continuing to work for Sutter.

As Sutter lost his workers to "gold fever," he soon found himself losing his land. Over the next several months, word of the gold discoveries spread far and wide. Men (and a few women) came from all over to try to strike it rich. As these newcomers dug up his land and slaughtered his cattle, Sutter found himself powerless to stop them. The fact that California had just been taken from Mexico by the United States added to the confusion over proper laws and procedures. Most likely, however, no laws would have been able to stop the rush of people looking for riches.

Sutter's Dream Ends

The gold strikes did increase Sutter's fame. In 1849, he became a delegate to California's constitutional convention. The following year, he ran for governor. He came in last in a three-person race, even finishing behind his former lawyer.

The years after the discovery of gold were difficult for John Sutter. The wife that Sutter had abandoned in Switzerland tracked him down and joined him in California. This was probably not a happy reunion for Sutter, who also had several children with a mistress who had traveled with him from Hawaii. With his business crumbling and his personal life falling apart, Sutter became a heavy drinker. This did not help him as he tried to protect what he had.

Sutter was never able to take advantage of his position as owner of the land near where gold was discovered (technically, Sutter's Mill was just outside his property). Instead of putting resources into finding gold himself, Sutter tried to maintain his previous business holdings. While he did make some money selling food and equipment to the new arrivals, he never earned the fortune that may have been waiting for him. He began selling his land and businesses and, by 1852, had gone bankrupt. The California government gave him a pension but by 1865, after a fire destroyed his farmhouse, Sutter left California for good.

Sutter spent the last 15 years of his life trying to convince Congress to compensate him for the money he lost because of the gold rush. Year after year, Sutter made the trip from Pennsylvania (where he lived) to Washington, DC, to ask Congress for money. Sutter died in 1880, just days after Congress had again refused his request for aid.

Legacy

One contemporary of Sutter remarked that "Marshall may have discovered the gold, but in a broader and grander sense . . . Sutter was the discoverer." This "great discovery" led to "a mass migration of people" to California and the West.

For most people who came to California in the 1850s, the discovery of gold at Sutter's Mill marked the beginning of a dream. But those people destroyed both Sutter's land and his plans for the future. Sutter's dreams died so that other people's dreams could live.

Quote is from John Bidwell, quoted in Lamar, Howard R., ed. *The New Encyclopedia of the American West*. Yale University Press, 1998.

James Marshall

(1810-1885)

The man who made one of the most important discoveries in California history began his life in 1810. James Marshall was the first child born to Philip and Sarah Marshall. James's parents, like their son, were born in New Jersey. In fact, James's great-grandfather represented New Jersey when he signed the Declaration of Independence.

James took after his father, a wagon maker, and became skilled in carpentry and woodworking. When his father beat James for shining his shoes on a Sunday (in violation of the Sabbath), James left home, never to return while his father was alive. Still a teenager, James worked in sawmills and did a variety of odd jobs, generally working with wood.

California

In 1837, Marshall headed west. He lived for several years in Missouri, farming and doing carpentry. Then he followed the Oregon Trail further west. By 1845 he had come to Sutter's Fort (near today's Sacramento) where he became one of the many skilled workers employed by John Sutter.

Marshall was soon able to buy some ranch property near Sutter. In 1846, he left his ranch to volunteer as part of John C. Frémont's force that fought Mexico for control of California. Marshall spent part of the Mexican War in the Los Angeles area, as a carpenter for the military authorities. By the time he returned to his property in 1847, other settlers had ruined it. People had taken his animals and destroyed much of his equipment. With little money, Marshall again turned to John Sutter.

A Great Discovery

Marshall and Sutter entered into a partnership to construct and run a gristmill and a sawmill. Sutter, who had the money, supplied labor and equipment. Marshall supervised construction and operation of the mills.

On January 24, 1848, Marshall was working on the millrace, the channel that takes water to the mill. On the bottom, where water had separated it from other sediment, lay Marshall's now famous discovery. Calling to his workers, he exclaimed, "By God, I think I've found a gold mine!"

Journeying through a harsh winter rain, Marshall hurried back to Sutter's Fort to consult with John Sutter. Using some scientific tests that they found in an encyclopedia, they confirmed that Marshall had discovered gold. A new chapter in California's history had begun.

Sutter's Mill in a New Era

This new chapter in California history was not a particularly successful one for James Marshall. Like his partner John Sutter, Marshall never turned his luck at being near the first gold strike into personal riches. Although he did some prospecting, it did not make him wealthy.

Marshall stayed at the mill and tried to make it profitable. Immediately, however, he ran into difficulties. His workers caught "gold fever." Many of them deserted the mill and went in search of gold. A flood damaged the sawmill later in the year. Marshall repaired and improved it and was soon producing wood for gold seekers and a profit.

This brief success did not last long. As people poured into the area, Marshall had to keep prospectors from destroying his land. He was faced with heavy debts and competition from other mills. By 1850, Sutter's Mill was closed.

Wanderings

Marshall's discovery brought him fame . . . but not fortune. As he searched for work, he found little sympathy and few jobs. "If I sought employment," he wrote in his journal, "I was refused on the reasoning that I had discovered the gold-mines and should be the one to employ them. . . Thus I wandered for more than four years."

Marshall's lack of success did little to improve his prickly personality. Already regarded as "odd" by many people who knew him, Marshall's unhappiness often made him angry as well. He became a heavy drinker and smoker and, by all accounts, was not a pleasant person.

In 1857, Marshall moved back near the Sutter's Mill area and started a vineyard. He had some success raising wine grapes and other fruit. For the next decade, Marshall made wine during the growing seasons and drank much of the rest of the time. He made some money but no fortune.

Later Marshall tried a variety of ways to support himself. He invested in a group that was mining quartz. He went on a lecture tour and told audiences of the moment when he discovered gold. He successfully lobbied the California legislature for a pension. He ran a blacksmith shop. He even worked as a gardener.

In 1885, the man who triggered the gold rush by his discovery died in his sleep. Much like John Sutter, his discovery made him a man who would be long remembered, but brought him no happiness or riches.

Quotes are from Lewis, Donovan. *Pioneers of California.* Scottwall Associates,1993.

John Bidwell

(1819-1900)

Few people were around to witness as many important
moments in California history as John Bidwell. Bidwell was
one of the first white Americans to settle in California, was
present as gold was discovered, and was there as California
grew during its first half-century of statehood. John Bidwell
became one of California's early success stories.

Early life

John Bidwell was born in Chautauqua County, New York in
1819. He was the second of five children born to Abram
and Clarissa Bidwell, although Abram had seven children
from a previous marriage. The Bidwell family had a long
history in America. John's ancestors had migrated to
Connecticut over one hundred years before.

In about 1829, Abram Bidwell moved his family to
Pennsylvania. Just five years later, they moved again, this
time to Ohio. While in Ohio, John Bidwell received a good
education, although he had to walk many miles to the school
where he studied. For a short time after he left school, John
worked as a teacher. Like many young men of his time,

however, Bidwell was attracted to the idea of exploring the West. In 1839, he moved to Missouri. His attempts to make it as a landowner there were not successful and, by 1841, he was ready to leave for California.

The Journey West

While in Missouri, John Bidwell became a member of the Western Emigration Society. Bidwell worked with the group to gather people for a journey over land to California. This was to be the first large group of settlers to travel from Missouri to California. Although such famous mountain men as Jedediah Smith had made the trip before, no settlers had made the overland journey to California.

The Bidwell-Bartleson party, named for Bidwell and the group's captain, John Bartleson, were fortunate to travel with another group headed for Oregon. That group had mountain man Thomas Fitzpatrick as their guide. This was important because none of the men and women of the Bidwell-Bartleson party had a very good sense of where they were going. "We only knew that California lay to the west," wrote Bidwell later. Combined with some maps of questionable accuracy, this ignorance would eventually get the group into trouble.

Bidwell's party followed the Oregon Trail as they made their way to California. In Idaho, they separated from those going to Oregon. The rest of the journey was a difficult and dangerous affair. Traveling through intense desert heat, they ran short of food and water. They were forced to eat many of their pack animals. Somehow, they made it to the San Joaquin Valley, where they met some Indians who gave them further directions. Weary and bedraggled, the group arrived at John Marsh's California ranch in November 1841.

The settlers had made history and paved a way for new migration. When John Bidwell's journal telling of his "successful" trip was published a few years later, many others decided to follow in his footsteps to California.

John Sutter

Bidwell soon became an important assistant and friend to John Sutter, working as a clerk at Sutter's Fort. During California's fight for independence from Mexico, Bidwell was an officer under Captain John C. Frémont. Soon after the discovery of gold at Sutter's Mill, Bidwell made his own gold discovery on the Feather River, at Bidwell's Bar. The income from his gold discoveries, combined with his ability to get a land grant for a ranch, gave Bidwell the tools he needed to become a wealthy man.

Successful Rancher

John Bidwell obtained a 22,000-acre ranch at Chico, not far from Sacramento. Using Indian labor like his friend Sutter, Bidwell turned his land into a center of agriculture in the

state. On his ranch, Bidwell raised poultry and sheep, cultivated grapes, and operated a sawmill. Bidwell lived to see the wheat that he produced declared the finest grain in the world at an international exhibition held in Paris.

Bidwell became a leading citizen in the state. Governor Leland Stanford appointed him a brigadier general in the state militia. Bidwell also served in Congress from 1864 to 1867 and lost a race for Governor in 1875. In 1892, he even ran for president as the candidate of the Prohibitionist party, which was best known for its opposition to alcohol.

Legacy

John Bidwell was one of the first Americans to arrive in California. Unlike most gold miners, he struck it rich in the gold fields. He became a wealthy rancher and political leader. When he died of a heart attack in 1900, John Bidwell had lived the life of a leader in California history.

Quote is from Lamar, Howard R., ed., *The New Encyclopedia of the American West.* Yale University Press, 1998.

Dame Shirley

[Louise Amelia Knapp Smith Clappe]
(1819-1906)

Today, historians can use all sorts of letters, records, notes, and objects to describe what the gold rush was like. But in Louise Clappe's day, it was hard to get the details. In 1851 and 1852, Louise Clappe wrote down her observations of the California mining camp where she lived. When her letters to her sister were published, they provided Americans of the day with one of the best descriptions of mining life. Even today, her words are read and her observations are still remembered.

Early Life and Education

Louise Amelia Knapp Smith was born in New Jersey in 1819. She was the first of seven children born to Lois and Moses Smith. Moses was a school director and education became very important in Louise's life. When Louise was seven or eight years old, her father moved the family to Massachusetts. Just five years later, Moses Smith died.

Louise received an excellent education for a young girl growing up in America. In most of the country, there was little public education, and little education in general for females. Fortunately for Louise, her teenage years came at a time in New England when people were experimenting with new ideas about the way society should work.

One of these reforms was the improvement of educational opportunities for young women. Louise attended several women's seminaries and received an education, not just in reading and writing, but in a wide variety of subjects. As she grew, Louise became a skilled writer, and often corresponded by letter.

Louise continued her education into her 20's, even after her mother died in 1837. She attended Amherst Academy in Massachusetts and spent most of the 1840s living in Amherst. During this time, she did some writing and spent a great deal of time traveling around New England seeing friends and relatives.

California

In 1849, Louise married a young doctor named Fayette Clapp and set sail for San Francisco. While the couple lived in the small but growing city, Louise Clappe (as she preferred to spell her name) began to sell things she wrote. A local newspaper published a number of letters and poems by the new Californian.

By 1851, Fayette decided that the young couple should leave San Francisco. City life did not agree with the doctor's poor health. Furthermore, Fayette had learned of the opportunity to be a physician at the Rich Bar mining area. This would enable Fayette both to use his skills as a doctor and, hopefully, to find some gold himself.

When Louise arrived at the mining settlement on Feather River Canyon, she entered an area where there were about 2,000 men and five women. The Clapps were far wealthier than were the average miners. In addition to living in a relatively comfortable cabin, Louise had servants to do her cleaning and cooking. At the Rich Bar and then later Indian Bar mining settlements, Louise put her time to good use and wrote the letters that would make "Dame Shirley" famous.

Letters from the Mines

From September 1851 until she left the mines in November of the following year, Louise Clappe penned 23 letters to her sister, describing what life was like in the mining camp. Although historians have no way of knowing for sure, it seems likely that when she wrote her letters she knew (or at least hoped) that they would someday be published.

Adopting the pen name of "Dame Shirley," Clappe constructed a detailed picture of mining life.

One of the things Clappe described was the beauty of her surroundings. The giant pine trees she encountered along the way to the camp, she wrote, "seem [to be] looking into Heaven itself." Clappe had briefly studied geology, but she confided to her sister, she "could never appreciate the poetry, or the humor, of making one's wrists ache by knocking to pieces gloomy looking stones..." Nevertheless, Clappe provided admiring and detailed descriptions of the world in which she lived.

But "Dame Shirley" was more interested in the people whose lives revolved around the search for gold. She described the conditions in which people lived and the dangers they faced. When a woman died at the camp, Clappe told of the funeral and of people's reactions. She also wrote of the first amputation that her husband had to perform while at the mines. In addition to writing of the crushed and diseased leg of the "Poor fellow," she also told of how her husband's reputation was on the line when he performed the ultimately successful operation.

Clappe wrote of the social conditions in the mining camp. She was particularly fond of the Mexican (she called them Spanish) prospectors who she believed were generally honorable and good workers. She was, however, critical of other immigrant groups and often surprised by the ways all of the miners behaved. "You know that at home it is considered *vulgar* for a gentleman to swear," she wrote her sister, "but I am told that here, it is absolutely the fashion."

Clappe criticized the violence that was part of mining life. In less than a month, Clappe reported to her sister in August 1852, "we have had murders, fearful accidents, bloody deaths, a mob, whippings, a hanging, an attempt at suicide, and a fatal duel." Despite her distaste for what had happened, it was important to Clappe to present the truth. "[I]f I leave out darker shades of our mountain life, the picture will be very incomplete."

By the time that she and her husband left Indian Bar at the end of 1852, Louise Clappe had presented one of the most complete pictures of mining life that had yet been written. By then, the gold in the area was exhausted and with the "failure of the golden harvest" the miners "left the river in crowds."

Back to Civilization

Shortly after returning to San Francisco in late 1852, Louise Clappe gave copies of the letters she had written to a friend who was starting a new literary magazine. The magazine's publishers hoped the *Pioneer* would be California's answer to the great magazines of New York. Dame Shirley's 23 letters were published, one in each issue, in the *Pioneer* magazine during 1854 and 1855. Few people knew that Louise Clappe was the true identity of Dame Shirley.

In 1854, Fayette claimed poor health and moved back to the East. By 1857, Louise and Fayette had divorced. Louise stayed in California and began a new profession as a schoolteacher. For the next 20 years, she taught school and fought to improve California's educational system. In 1859, after her sister Henrietta died, she took charge of her young niece Genevieve.

Legacy

Louise Clappe retired from teaching in 1878 and moved to New York. She continued lecturing and writing. Near the turn-of-the-century, she moved to a retirement home in New Jersey, where she died in 1906.

Dame Shirley's writing entertained and educated Americans of her time and in the years since. Famous writers, including historian Hubert Howe Bancroft and short story author Bret Harte, used her words as source material for their writings. In 1922, her letters were collected and published as a book, ensuring that they would educate generations to come.

Quotes are from Clappe, Louise Amelia Knapp Smith. *The Shirley Letters from the California Mines, 1851-1852*. Heyday Books, 1998.

Charles Christian Nahl

(1818-1878)

When we imagine the gold rush we often picture the dusty 49er panning for gold and living his difficult life. In many ways, a German artist was responsible for creating this image of California during the gold rush.

Germany

Charles Christian Nahl was born in Kassel, Germany, the first child of Fritz and Henrietta Nahl. For 200 years, members of the Nahl family had been craftsmen, painters, and artists. Charles seemed destined to follow that path.

Although as a youth he loved to raise horses, Nahl quickly became an eager art student. Many members of his family, including his father, tutored him in art. He also attended art schools where he developed his skills and technique.

Despite his growing talent, Nahl's childhood was not a particularly happy one. His parents divorced in 1826 and his mother soon married Fritz's cousin. Nahl grew to become a professional artist in Germany. By 1846, he was ready to begin a new life in Paris.

Transitions

In 1846, Nahl moved to Paris with a friend and five of his relatives, including his mother and his half-brother Hugo. Although Paris was a center of art and culture, Nahl did not stay there long. France's poor economy made it difficult to make much money as an artist. One of his clients was a ship's captain who was going to America. The two made a deal. In exchange for Nahl's portrait of the captain, the captain's ship would take Nahl and his family to America.

Nahl arrived in New York in 1849. He enjoyed the city and felt that it was a good place to be an artist. His family, however, had once been extremely wealthy. The possibility of earning a fortune prospecting for gold in California convinced Nahl to move his family once again. The difficult journey took about two months, traveling mainly by boat and using the route that went over land across the Isthmus of Panama. The Nahls arrived in San Francisco in May 1851.

Mining camps

After a brief stop at Nevada City, the Nahls settled at the Rough and Ready mining camp. This is the camp where young Lotta Crabtree made her dancing and singing debut. Unlike the Nahl family, most miners were not well educated. Nahl's large tent, filled with things like a suit of chain mail armor, made others consider him somewhat strange.

Nahl quickly discovered that he was unlikely to make much money looking for gold. The family turned to other pursuits. As Dame Shirley recalled, his mother Henrietta became a camp washerwoman. Nahl went back to using his artistic talents. His sketches of the miners were popular and important. For the price of a brief sketch, miners could have a record of themselves in California that they could send to friends and family back home.

Sacramento

By the end of 1851, Nahl had moved to Sacramento and opened an art studio. He worked on all types of art there, including paintings and wood engravings. But his most popular product was the illustrations he drew for newspapers. Working from his memory of the gold fields, Nahl created dozens of images of mining life. Like his other sketches, these newspaper pictures became extremely popular items for miners and others to send back home. One writer has called them "California's first picture postcards."

San Francisco

In 1852, Nahl moved his studio to San Francisco. In the growing city, he became known as one of the best artists of gold rush life. Nahl took photographs, drew sketches, painted portraits, and etched newspaper illustrations. His drawings are the most remembered images of the famous bandit Joaquín Murieta. Nahl also became involved in city politics. In a time in which there was no real police force and a growing fear of crime, Nahl worked with the "committee of vigilance" who appointed themselves in charge of law and order.

Later Life

Nahl lived in San Francisco until his death from typhoid fever in 1878. In 1867, his work attracted the attention of the wealthy Judge E. B. Crocker. Crocker commissioned Nahl to create several paintings including "Sunday Morning in the Mines." Here Nahl painted a giant canvas showing a mining scene in which some miners were quiet Sabbath followers and others were wild and unruly. This work, like so many of Nahl's paintings, showed the mix of people and ideas in a mining town.

Legacy

Charles Christian Nahl's artistic talent and familiarity with the gold rush made him one of the most important artists in the history of California. In works like "Miners in the Sierras," "Fire in San Francisco Bay," and "Saturday Evening in the Mines," he created an image of California and the gold rush that would remain until this day.

Quote is from Stevens, Moreland L. *Charles Christian Nahl: Artist of the Gold Rush, 1818-1878.* [exhibition catalogue] E.B. Crocker Art Gallery, 1976.

Joaquín Murieta
(1830?-1853? or 1830-1878)

A legend is a story that may be based on actual historical events but, over time, has become practically impossible to prove or disprove. Nevertheless, many people believe legends, and the stories themselves become more important then what actually happened.

The story of Joaquín Murieta is one of the great legends of California. Some historians argue that he never existed. The story of Murieta, they say, is really a combination of many tales of gold rush California. Most who have studied the subject, however, believe that there was a bandit named Murieta (or something like it) who lived in California during the early part of the gold rush. While we may never know all of the actual details of his life, Joaquín Murieta, and the image he represents, is an important part of California history.

Youth

Joaquín Murieta was born about 1830 in Sonora, Mexico. His father is believed to have been of Mayo Indian descent and his mother may have been Spanish. Murieta received an education at a Jesuit school in Mexico. Little is known about his youth but sources agree that he became a miner in California shortly after the beginning of the gold rush.

Prejudice

As Americans rushed to California in search of gold they discovered many people of Mexican heritage already there. The white Americans' fear of competition was added to their prejudice against people with darker skin. In response, the California Legislature passed the "Foreign Miners Tax of 1850." Officially, this law meant that all miners who were not Americans would pay a large tax for the right to mine. In reality, the law was mainly enforced against Mexicans. The thousands of whites who came from Canada and Europe were allowed to mine without paying the tax.

Some Mexicans who were not allowed to mine felt forced to turn to a life of crime. They became horse thieves, cattle rustlers, and armed robbers. By most accounts, Joaquín Murieta was one of these bandits. He became a feared figure in California.

Capture?

By 1853, attacks on settlers and their possessions were causing major concern. Newspapers such as the *San Joaquin Republican* began demanding that the state take action against the outlaws. The California Legislature hired Texas Ranger Harry Love to capture five outlaws, all known as "Joaquín." Love and his men were told to capture Joaquín Botellier, Joaquín Carillo, Joaquín Ocomorenia, Joaquín Valenzuela, and Joaquín Muriati. Muriati may have been an alternate spelling for Murieta (or Murrieta, as it is sometimes spelled). In addition to the salary promised by the Legislature, Governor John Bigler offered a $1000 reward for capturing one of the outlaws.

Love's group spent the next few months searching for the Joaquíns and harassing men of Mexican heritage. On July 25th, right before Love's contract with the government was going to expire, Love's Rangers battled a group of Mexicans near Tulare Plains. In the fight, Love's party killed two men. They soon identified the first man as Manuel García, better known as the outlaw Tres Dedos, or Three-Fingered Jack. They claimed that the second man they killed was the bandit Joaquín Murieta. As evidence, Love's men cut off Murieta's head and placed it in a glass container filled with whiskey to preserve it.

Reaction

Soon after, the debate began on whether Love had really killed Murieta. Love got a number of men to swear that the person captured was really Joaquín Murieta, the famous bandit. Love's word was apparently good enough for the Legislature and the governor. The head was considered proof of Murieta's death, and the Legislature voted for an additional payment of $5,000 for Love and his men.

Not everyone was convinced that a terrible bandit had been killed. In August 1853, the *San Francisco Alta* proclaimed the story "humbug" (an old word for "false" or "not believable"). Many miners and other Californians, however, continued to believe that Murieta had been captured. The head, preserved in alcohol, was brought to the mining camps in central California where people paid $1 each to see it.

Murieta's Final Demise

Joaquín Murieta (assuming he existed at all) probably died on that day in 1853. Other stories, however, say that he moved back to Mexico and lived the quiet life of a rancher for the next 25 years. In any case, "Murieta's head" became an attraction at a San Francisco museum where it remained until its destruction in the great earthquake and fire of 1906.

The Story Lives On

Despite Murieta's apparent death in 1853, his importance as a California figure continued to grow. The story of Joaquín Murieta was told again and again, each time with new additions and interpretations of the man's life.

The man who first made Joaquín Murieta famous was a Cherokee Indian named John Ridge. Ridge portrayed Murieta as a Robin Hood-type figure. According to Ridge, Murieta was driven to a life of crime after whites killed his brother and attacked other members of his family. By this account, Murieta was not evil, but was in fact avenging the wrongs committed upon him by others. Furthermore, Murieta was not a lone outlaw or a man who traveled with a small group of companions. According to Ridge, Murieta was the brave leader of thousands of men. Writing under the name Yellow Bird, Ridge published the *Life and Adventures of Joaquín Murieta* in 1854. His writing would become the basis of the legend of Joaquín Murieta.

Ridge was not the only person to tell the story of the famous bandit. Tales of Murieta spread all the way to Europe and South America. Independent versions of the story appeared in Spain and France. Another story was told in Chile, in which Murieta was no longer a Mexican but in fact a Chilean bandit.

In 1859, the *California Police Gazette* published its own version of Murieta's life. This version became important for the illustrations by artist Charles Christian Nahl. Soon, Murieta's story became a popular San Francisco play. In the play, Murieta sees a sign offering a $5,000 reward for his capture and, with heroic daring, signs his name to it and writes "I will give $10,000." In the 1880s, California historian Hubert Howe Bancroft retold the Murieta story.

Murieta's story has continued to be popular in the 20th century. In 1932, a version of the story called Murieta the *Robin Hood of El Dorado*. Four years later, a movie was based on the book. In more recent years, the award-winning poet Pablo Neruda wrote a play about Murieta.

Legacy

The story of Joaquín Murieta has become one of the most famous tales of gold rush era California. Whether he was a vicious bandit, a cultural hero, or simply a wronged man (or even if he ever existed) remains in dispute. Clearly, though, Murieta's story will forever remain part of the legacy of the California gold rush.

Quote is from Joseph Henry Jackson's introduction to Ridge, John Rollin. *The Life and Adventures of Joaquín Murieta, the Celebrated California Bandit*. University of Oklahoma Press, 1955.

John Rollin Ridge

(1827-1867)

The tale of the famous outlaw Joaquín Murieta was one of the best-known stories to come out of California's gold rush. John Rollin Ridge was the man most responsible for spreading that story. Using his skill as a writer, Ridge drew a picture for Americans of an exciting and dangerous West.

Youth

John Rollin Ridge was born in Georgia in 1827. His mother was white, and his father was Cherokee Indian. John's grandfather Major Ridge and father John Ridge were part of a small group of Cherokee leaders who hoped that signing a treaty with the United States government would help protect the Cherokee nation. These few Cherokee leaders weakened Cherokee resistance to the American attempts to force the Cherokee to leave Georgia. In 1838-39, Cherokees were forced west in a march along what became known as of the "trail of tears." John's father was killed by Cherokees who blamed him for signing the treaty.

John, at age 12, was sent to New England to get an education but soon returned to the family's new home in

Arkansas. A few years later, Ridge got into a fight and killed a man, probably in self-defense. Fearing further violence or arrest, Ridge escaped to Missouri. By the end of the 1840s he heard about gold in California. Looking for a new life, in 1850 Ridge joined a company that was headed to California to strike it rich in the mines.

California

Ridge soon discovered the difficulties of mining life. Like so many of his fellows, he was not very successful as a prospector. Writing to a friend in 1853 he complained, "I have worked harder than any slave I ever owned, or my father either. All to no purpose. I have tried the mines, I have tried trading, I have tried everything, but to no avail..."

Fortunately for Ridge, he had other skills. He could earn money as a writer. Ridge wrote newspaper articles and stories for the *Pioneer*, a new magazine that would become known for publishing Dame Shirley's *Letters from the Mines*. Ridge published poems and short stories in California and even made money writing letters describing mining conditions for a newspaper in New Orleans.

Joaquín Murieta

In 1854, Ridge wrote the book that made him famous: *The Life and Adventures of Joaquín Murieta*. He used a translation of his Indian name, Yellow Bird. Ridge was a professional writer but his skill was in writing fiction, not history. He knew that people were fascinated by tales of famous bandits and that Texas Ranger Harry Love's capture of a man believed to be Murieta had excited people all over California.

Ridge's story was probably a combination of fact, personal experience, and outright fiction. Clearly, as Ridge described, there were many bandits who operated in California gold country. Most believed that Joaquín Murieta was one of them and that he was killed by Harry Love. Much of Ridge's story, however, contains things that Murieta supposedly said. There is no reason to believe that Ridge could have learned of Murieta's exact words. Working with very little actual information about Murieta, Ridge created a picture of a dashing, daring thief.

Ridge based his description of Murieta on the famous English bandit Robin Hood. Robin Hood was known as a great leader of men who became an outlaw because he was badly treated. Like Robin Hood, the Murieta that Ridge described was treated poorly by the authorities. California law prevented him from gold mining because he was Mexican.

In addition, Murieta faced much violence living in California. According to Ridge, white men attacked members of Murieta's family and killed his brother. In addition, Murieta himself was beaten and whipped.

While we do not know if a person named Joaquín Murieta really had all these things happen to him, we do know that things like this did happen in California. California during the gold rush was often a very dangerous place, especially for people of Mexican heritage.

According to Ridge, Murieta was brave and honorable and the leader of thousands of men. Like Robin Hood, the noble bandit had a good reason for going outside the law and plotting his revenge. This version of Joaquín Murieta's story is the one that is still known today.

Legacy

Although John Ridge was successful in spreading an exciting story about a dashing bandit, he did not make as much money doing so as he had hoped. This story was so popular that soon others were writing it, too. Ridge helped the South during the Civil War and later published a book of poems. His tales of the famous bandit Joaquín Murieta, however, will be the reason that he and Murieta are long remembered.

Quote is from Joseph Henry Jackson's introduction to Ridge, John Rollin. *The Life and Adventures of Joaquín Murieta, the Celebrated California Bandit.* University of Oklahoma Press, 1955.

Lotta Crabtree

(1847-1924)

During the gold rush, many people came to California seeking wealth and fame. Most of those people were men who hoped that they would find gold and become rich. A number of women and children also came to California during the gold rush. One of these children, Lotta Crabtree, did indeed strike it rich in California. While she did not prospect for gold, she became more successful than all but a handful of gold seekers.

Lotta Crabtree was born in New York City in 1847. Her father, John Crabtree, decided to give up his business selling books and look for gold in California. In 1853, Lotta and her mother, Mary Ann Crabtree, made the trip west and joined John in Grass Valley, California.

Child Star

Upon her arrival, little Lotta met her famous neighbor, Lola Montez. Montez was a dancer whose "spider dance," a loose copy of the famous Tarantella, was as popular with the miners as it had been when Montez danced in Europe. Montez, who passed herself off as a Spanish beauty, was actually an Irish woman who had long ago changed her name.

Child performers were extremely popular in California. Miners appreciated entertainment that could bring much-needed fun into their lonely lives. Montez's great success as an entertainer gave Mary Ann the idea that her sweet-voiced daughter could also become a celebrity. Montez helped tutor Lotta in her dancing and stage presence, and the young girl entered a local dancing school.

Lotta made her grand stage debut when she was almost eight years old. Accompanied by Lola Montez, Lotta went to the Rough and Ready mining camp in Rabbit Creek. Lotta sang for the miners and danced an Irish jig. The miners loved the bubbly little girl's performance and her happy-go-lucky attitude. When the show was done, they threw pieces of gold to her in appreciation. A star had been born.

Lotta learned new songs and dances and became known as "the airy, fairy, singing, dancing, miners' darling." She began to tour the area, performing in camps for the miners.

Her mother, who soon devoted herself full-time to managing her daughter's career, arranged for people to play the guitar and the violin to accompany Lotta's singing.

Lotta toured California for years, delighting miners with her stage act. In 1859, she moved to San Francisco. The adolescent star was as big of a hit in the growing city of San Francisco as she had been in the rougher mining communities. Lotta sang in many music halls and theaters throughout the city. As she played and sang, her reputation grew. Lotta's California career ended at the age of 17 when, after performing in a charity concert that earned $1500, she and her mother set off for New York.

National Sensation

Lotta was surely the first major national and international sensation to come out of California's rough environment. Based in New York, Lotta became an even bigger star. She continued to sing and dance in front of large audiences throughout the United States and in large European cities like London.

She also became a famous and successful actress. Lotta acted in many plays, including some based on the work of famous authors like Charles Dickens. She became so well known and respected, in fact, that people wrote plays for her to star in. Lotta Crabtree, young California singer and dancer, became the highest paid actress in the country.

Lotta Crabtree became a successful businesswoman with her own touring company. This gave her (and her mother) a great deal of control over her career and finances. It also helped ensure that she would continue to be the person who got the money earned by her singing and acting.

Lotta's personal life was shaped by her relationship with her mother. She never married, even though she once became engaged to an army officer. Her mother's disapproval, however, broke the engagement. When Mary Ann Crabtree got older, Lotta cared for her until she died in 1905.

Legacy

Lotta made a brief return to San Francisco in 1875. There, the internationally famous star donated a cast-iron fountain to the city. "Lotta's Fountain" was erected on Market Street, San Francisco's main thoroughfare. The fountain survived the 1906 earthquake and fire, and became a popular meeting place in the city.

Lotta retired from her professional career in 1891. She lived with relatives and had a life of great ease. When she died in 1924, she left all of her money to charity. By that time, she had a fortune of $4,000,000, a staggering amount of money in those days. She had come a long way from the mining village where she made her stage debut.

Quote is from Altman, Linda Jacobs. *The California Gold Rush in American History.* Enslow, 1997.

"Snowshoe" Thompson
(1827-1876)

Life was difficult for gold miners. The miners were mostly single men, or men away from their families. They were lonely. Miners spent day after day hoping to strike it rich. Few of them ever did.

In sparsely populated areas like the region directly east of the Sierra Nevada Mountains, miners had little contact with the outside world. Mail service was their only link to civilization. Only by mail could miners communicate with their families, get news, and conduct business. Getting mail, however, was not easy. "Snowshoe" Thompson became a local hero because he brought mail to lonely miners and others east of the Sierra Nevada.

"Snowshoe"

John Albert Thompson was born in the mountainous Telemark region of Norway in 1827. He traveled with his family to the United States as a child and settled in the Midwest. He moved to California around the age of 24, and became a miner and a rancher in the Sacramento Valley.

In 1856, Thompson answered an advertisement in a Sacramento newspaper. Someone was needed to deliver the mail in the Sierra Nevada Mountain region. While the mountains were extremely difficult to cross, particularly in winter, the Norwegian Thompson was positive he could make the dangerous passage successfully.

Thompson built himself a set of skis similar to those used in his home region of Norway. Ten feet long and four inches wide, these skis enabled Thompson to travel great distances over rough terrain. He called these skis his snowshoes and the legend of "Snowshoe" Thompson was born.

Thompson's fame grew later that year when he made a daring rescue. Around Christmas 1856, Thompson discovered a local trapper named James Sisson on the verge of freezing to death. Thomson skied from Nevada across the

Sierra and eventually all the way to Sacramento. Upon obtaining the needed medical supplies in Sacramento, Thompson went all the way back to Genoa, Nevada. Having covered about 400 miles in ten days, Thompson was rewarded with knowing that he had saved Sisson's life.

Although most of his trips were not as dramatic, every journey Thompson took from Placerville to Genoa (his main mail route) was an adventure. He made several trips a year, often through conditions that most would have found impassible. His mail route also took him between many local mining camps and settlements. In this way, Thompson linked miners with each other and with the outside world.

On the Trails

Thompson carried heavy loads on his journeys. In addition to letters, Thompson carried all sorts of other things. He brought badly needed medicine to miners and others. He also brought a variety of supplies that people needed, including clothes and metal pots and pans. At times, Thompson's pack weighed as much as 100 pounds.

In contrast to the great amounts that Thompson carried for others, he brought very few things for himself on his journeys. He carried with him no food that needed to be cooked and often no water. Instead, he took only dried, salted meat (which stays well preserved) and some bread. He melted snow for drinking water.

Amazingly, Thomson brought almost as little clothing with him as he did food. "Snowshoe" did not want to be slowed down by the bulky clothing people used to keep warm. At great risk to himself, his Mackinaw jacket was (along with a hat) his main piece of cold-weather clothing. Thomson's activity kept him warm while he was moving and he managed to avoid frostbite while asleep.

A few of his trips became famous. In 1859, Thompson carried some rock from Nevada to Sacramento to be tested for silver. The discovery of silver soon brought a "silver rush" to Nevada's Comstock Lode. Thompson made another famous trip when he went to Washington, DC, to ask for federal pay for his work in providing mail service. When his train broke down in Laramie, Wyoming, Thomson walked the 50 miles to Cheyenne and caught another train. The U.S. government refused his request.

Legacy

Thompson made mail runs for the rest of his life, for a total of twenty years. The blond Norwegian with flowing hair was often seen engaging in one of his favorite hobbies: ski jumping. He was said to have been able to jump almost 200 feet. As he got older, he became involved in local Nevada politics. Snowshoe Thompson died in Genoa, Nevada, in 1876. The town now holds a festival in memory of the Norwegian mail carrier whose skill and daring were greatly valued by many a miner during the gold rush.

Mary Ellen Pleasant

(1814?-1904)

Much about Mary Ellen Pleasant remains a mystery. Historians have not yet been able to reconstruct all of the details of her life. However, what we know proves that she was an extraordinary person. Living in a city dominated by white men, she succeeded while being neither white nor male. Also, she managed to balance her desire for money (which, after all, was most people's goal) with a desire to do good things.

Out of Slavery

Mary Ellen Pleasant was born a slave in Georgia around 1814. Her mother was a slave who had been brought to Georgia from Haiti. Her father was a slave owner who was the son of Virginia's governor. Like many children of mixed race born while slavery dominated the South, Mary Ellen legally became the property of her father.

When Pleasant was about nine years old, her freedom was purchased and she was sent to Massachusetts. There she became an indentured servant to a Quaker family. As an indentured servant, she was not quite a slave, but she was also not allowed to pursue her own path. Nevertheless, she did much during this period in her life. The Quaker family for whom she worked strongly opposed slavery. Pleasant became acquainted with many of the leaders of the abolitionist (against slavery) cause. Soon, she would be doing her own work to aid African-Americans in distress.

Underground Railroad

Pleasant completed the terms of her indenture sometime around 1841 and became fully free. She married a wealthy abolitionist who was also of mixed race. This was important because both of them were able to "pass" as whites, which made it easier for them to help escaped slaves.

The couple worked together on the Underground Railroad, helping slaves who had escaped from their owners in the South make their way north. They would provide food, shelter, directions, and protection. This was difficult and dangerous work, not to mention illegal at a time when slavery was still the law throughout the South. When Pleasant's identity as a "conductor" on the Underground Railroad was discovered around 1850, she was forced to escape to avoid prosecution. By 1852, she had started a new life in California.

California Businesswoman

Pleasant earned a great deal of money in California. She became a well-known figure in San Francisco, running boarding houses in which many rich men stayed. San Francisco was a town of great wealth but few families, and many people had not set up households of their own. This made the boarding house business an important one.

Because she often met with rich and powerful people who stayed in her boarding houses, Pleasant had many important friends in San Francisco. She used her wealth and contacts in a variety of ways.

In San Francisco, Pleasant continued to help escaped slaves. Even though California had been admitted into the United States as a free state, the national fugitive slave law made it illegal to help people who had escaped from slavery. Pleasant worked to shelter these people from authorities, and help find them jobs and homes.

Pleasant also worked to help women in distress. Providing similar services for poor white women as she did for fugitive slaves, Pleasant helped many women to escape abusive husbands to find jobs.

Civil Rights Activist

Pleasant was not loved by everyone in San Francisco society. Many people claimed that her wealth came not just from boarding houses, but from houses of prostitution. The women she "saved," Pleasant's opponents said, were not being saved at all. Pleasant also sometimes used rich people's secrets against them, to raise money or get favors.

Pleasant's friends and enemies could agree on one thing: she was a strong fighter for the things she believed in. In 1858, Pleasant traveled east and lent personal and financial support to the abolitionist John Brown. Brown's unsuccessful attempt to trigger a slave rebellion and his later execution were important events leading to the Civil War.

Pleasant returned to California and continued her fight for equal rights. She was a founding member of the Franchise League that worked to overturn a California law that forbade blacks to testify in court cases with whites. That fight was won in 1863. Pleasant also fought successfully to end discrimination against blacks on public trolleys.

Legacy

Pleasant lived a long life as a California businesswoman and political activist. When she died in 1904, she had gained (and mostly lost) a sizable fortune. Although details of her life remain mysterious, it is clear that she was a significant figure in California history. The woman who was insultingly called "Mammy" because of her race made significant contributions to the causes of freedom and equal treatment for black Americans.

Levi Strauss
(1830?-1902)

The prospectors during the gold rush did rough work. Often up to their ankles in water or dirt, they spent their days outside, looking for those nuggets that would change their lives. Among the many difficulties they faced was a lack of sturdy clothing to wear as they did their dirty job. A Jewish immigrant from Germany would help solve that problem and, in the process, become famous the entire world over.

Early Life

Levi Strauss was born in Bavaria (a region of Germany) in about 1830. He was the second child of Hirsch Strauss and Rebecca Strauss (whose maiden name was Haas). His father was a dry goods salesman and peddler. He traveled from town to town and door to door selling a variety of products that would not spoil, such as clothes. His father died from tuberculosis in 1845 and, in 1847, Levi and his brothers left Germany and traveled to New York City.

In New York Levi joined his brothers in a dry goods business. Much as his father had done in Germany, Strauss carried goods like buttons, shoes, and linens with him as he

looked for customers. For a time, he worked in Kentucky.
Sometime in the early 1850s, Strauss went to San Francisco.

From Peddler to Merchant

Unlike so many people who came to California at this time,
Strauss had no interest in searching for gold. He did,
however, hope to profit from the gold rush. San Francisco
was a "boom town" at that time. Many people were
arriving, and there were not enough supplies. For that
reason, clothes, tools, and food items were very expensive.

Strauss arrived in San Francisco with a variety of goods
from his brothers' New York store. He was able to sell most
of the items quickly, at very good prices. One thing that
Strauss did not sell quickly was the canvas that he had
brought so that the miners could make tents. According to
legend, inspiration struck when Strauss had a conversation
with a prospector who complained about the low quality of
the pants that he and his fellows had to wear when they were
in the gold fields. Strauss used the canvas to make a sturdier
pair of pants for the man. The new pants were a big success
and soon prospectors all over California wanted these
"wonderful pants of Levi's" for themselves.

Strauss soon had a strong business in the gold fields. Using
a wagon to travel with his products, Strauss sold supplies
that he got from his brothers in New York to businesses and
stores throughout the gold country. But despite his success

selling other products, his pants (which soon became known as Levi's) became the center of his business. Soon, the success of "Levi's" enabled Strauss to leave the gold fields and set up a shop in San Francisco.

Wealthy Businessman

Strauss's business expanded greatly over the next few decades because of some good decisions that Levi and his partners (mainly his brothers) made. Strauss wanted to find a better fabric to make his pants than the tent canvas that he first used. He found the answer in a French cotton that was called, in English, *denim*. This was more comfortable than canvas, and would shrink to fit the proportions of its wearer. The cotton was dyed blue using indigo, a plant grown in South Carolina and other places. Strauss also obtained a patent, with another partner, on copper rivets that could be used to help fasten these "blue jeans" together at places where they could otherwise tear.

Strauss made his most important decision in the 1860s when he decided to build a factory in San Francisco. Previously, his brothers had supplied the jeans from the East. In 1867, Strauss opened his factory in San Francisco on Battery

Street, the same location that is still the company headquarters today. By the 1890s, the business was taking in one million dollars a year.

Later Life

Levi Strauss never married. He once told an interviewer that his "entire life is my business." Despite this focus on his company, Strauss was not solely interested in becoming wealthy. "I do not think large fortunes cause happiness to their owners, for immediately those who possess them become slaves to their wealth." Strauss donated money to many charities, including a number of them that had a Jewish focus. He became known for his strong financial support to the University of California. His heirs in the business, the Haas family, continued that support.

Legacy

When one hears the name Levi Strauss today, one probably does not think of a man but rather of a pair of jeans. That shows the success of Levi Strauss, the businessman. Without the gold rush, Levi's great success would not have been possible. When we put on a pair of jeans today, we can remember that they are another contribution to the world of the California gold rush.

Quote on page 57 is from Lamar, Howard R., ed. *The New Encyclopedia of the American West*. Yale University Press, 1998.
Quote on page 58 is from Van Steenwyk, Elizabeth. *Levi Strauss: The Blue Jeans Man*. Walker, 1988.

Domingo Ghirardelli
(1817-1894)

Chocolate. For miners and others in gold rush California, chocolate was one of the few delicacies available to them. One man, still known for that delicious product today, became the reason why miners could lick their lips in anticipation when hearing the word: chocolate.

Early Life

Domingo Ghirardelli was born in Italy in 1817. His father was a successful *chocolatier* (maker of chocolate) and candymaker. When he was 19, Domingo moved to Peru and began his own successful business making candy. He was lucky to have James Lick as a neighbor. Lick was an American-born piano maker who operated a shop near Ghirardelli's and told Ghirardelli of America. Lick moved to San Francisco in 1848 and became a very successful and wealthy merchant in the city.

California

Excited by Lick's tales of success in the booming gold rush town, Ghirardelli joined his old friend in the United States in

1849. There, Ghirardelli tried all sorts of ways to make money. Like so many newcomers to California, Ghirardelli tried his hand at prospecting for gold. When he failed to get rich this way, he tried operating a hotel, running a restaurant, and working as a storekeeper. Only when he returned to the business that had made his family successful did he strike it rich in California.

Chocolate

Although Domingo Ghirardelli brought his chocolate making experience from Europe, chocolate originally came from the New World. Cacao trees grow naturally in Central America and the regions surrounding it. When Spanish explorers came to Mexico in the 1500s, they learned of this delicious plant from the people they encountered. Chocolate played an important role in the Aztec and Inca civilizations and was popular as both a drink and, when sweetened, just to eat.

Setting up Shop

Domingo Ghirardelli realized that chocolate could become a valuable object among the miners. While it probably could not be used as money, as it once was in Mexico, it could become very popular as a dessert item. Ghirardelli began a business selling food and equipment to prospectors who were working in California's gold fields. One of the items that he sold was the chocolate that he had learned to make as a child.

The business became extremely successful. Within a few years of his arrival in California, Ghirardelli had about $25,000. This made him one of the wealthier men in California. With this great success, Ghirardelli moved his business from the mining areas to San Francisco. By this time (the early 1850s), his friend and fellow San Franciscan James Lick was almost a millionaire. Soon, Ghirardelli was on his way to that type of success.

Ghirardelli Chocolate

Although he started his business closer to the gold country, Ghirardelli grew his empire in San Francisco, where he started a chocolate factory. The factory was moved several times over the course of Ghirardelli's life, and the business kept growing. Even after Domingo died in 1894, the business continued to flourish. The following year the Ghirardelli chocolate factory moved into the location that would become the company's longtime home.

Future generations of Ghirardellis took over where Domingo left off. The business expanded and Ghirardelli chocolate is now known throughout the world. Ghirardelli Square is named after the famous chocolate manufacturer and hosts not only the chocolate factory but also a variety of restaurants and shops. Ghirardelli Square is now one of San Francisco's most popular tourist attractions.

Legacy

Domingo Ghirardelli's life shows several things about the people of the gold rush and how the time influenced America. Domingo, an Italian who had lived in Peru, came to this country because of the gold rush. The lure of gold brought many people with different talents and experiences to California. While most of them came in search of gold, many discovered that there were other ways to prosper from the gold rush environment. Domingo succeeded not when he searched for gold, as a lucky few did, but when he used the knowledge he already had about making chocolate and candy and applied it to a new time and place.

Like Levi Strauss and Company, Ghirardelli Chocolate became one of a number of successful businesses started in the gold rush.

For More Information

Altman, Linda Jacobs. *The California Gold Rush in American History*. ("In American History" series). Enslow, 1997.

Bibbs, Susheel. *Heritage of Power (Marie LaVeau/Mary Ellen Pleasant)*. MEP Publications, 1998.

Clappe, Louise Amelia Knapp Smith. *The Shirley Letters from the California Mines, 1851-1852*. Heyday Books, 1998.

Holliday, J.S. *Rush for Riches: Gold Fever and the Making of California*. University of California Press, 1999.

Ketchum, Liza. *The Gold Rush*. Little, Brown, 1996.

Lamar, Howard R., ed. *The New Encyclopedia of the American West*. Yale University Press, 1998. (Adult reference source)

Levy, Joann. *They Saw the Elephant: Women in the California Gold Rush*. Archon Books, 1990.

Ridge, John Rollin. *The Life and Adventures of Joaquín Miller, the Celebrated California Bandit*. University of Oklahoma Press, 1955.

Sherrow, Victoria. *Life During the Gold Rush*. ("The Way People Live" series). Lucent Books, 1998.

Van Steenwyk, Elizabeth. *Levi Strauss: The Blue Jeans Man*. Walker, 1988.

About the Author

Adam D. Parker is a writer and editor who studied history as an undergraduate at the University of California at Berkeley and earned a Masters degree in history at the University of Wisconsin-Madison. An avid baseball fan and bridge player, Adam lives with his wife and their dog in the San Francisco Bay Area.